UNSTOPPABLE HOPE

Unstoppable HOPE

An 18-Day Journey To Renew The HOPE Within.

DeMarlo McKinney

© 2015 DeMarlo McKinney
All rights reserved. This book is protected by the copyright laws of the United States of America. No portion of this book may be reproduced, stored in a retrieval or transmitted in and form or by any means-electronic, mechanical, photocopy, recording, scanning, or other-except for brief quotations in critical reviews or articles, without the prior written permission of the publisher.
Scriptures quotations marked NLT are take from the Holy Bible, New Living Translation, copyright 1996, 2004.
Scriptures quotations marked NASB are taken from the NEW AMERICAN STANDARD BIBLE, © 1960, 1962, 1963, 1968, 1971, 1972, 1973, 1975, 1977, 1995. Scriptures quotations marked KJV are taken from the King James Version.

Cover Design By Wolf Pack Visions

ISBN-13:
978-0692465257 (The HOPE Coach Publications)

ISBN-10:
0692465251

Dedication

This book is dedicated to my incredible, loving and amazing wife Kriston Nicole. I am who I am today because God sent you into my life at the tender age of eight years old. From that point to now you have made a tremendous impact on me, one that can never be reversed. Thank you for believing in me even when I didn't. Thank you for your continuous push for excellence and never letting me settle for mediocrity. The Lord used you to teach me the true meaning of integrity. You are an amazing mother to our son and, I'm honored to pastor with you and be your partner in life. I love you! Lets change the world together. You are my hero.

CONTENTS

Day One	HOPE'S Definition
Day Two	HOPE'S Belief
Day Three	HOPE'S Expectation
Day Four	HOPE'S Focus
Day Five	HOPE'S Attitude
Day Six	HOPE'S Confidence
Day Seven	HOPE'S Confession
Day Eight	HOPE'S Scriptures
Day Nine	HOPE'S Cleansing
Day Ten	HOPE'S Anger
Day Eleven	HOPE'S Courage
Day Twelve	HOPE'S Joy
Day Thirteen	HOPE'S Peace
Day Fourteen	HOPE'S Perspective
Day Fifteen	HOPE Dealer
Day Sixteen	HOPE'S Foundation
Day Seventeen	Unstoppable HOPE
Day Eighteen	Declarations of HOPE

Day 1

HOPE'S Definition

HOPE – The Belief and Expectation that Things will change.

    I've come to declare to you today, that things will change! Often times we hear people say, "I hope" or "Hopefully." As if they are trying to convince themselves of the change. When HOPE shows up in your life it comes with confidence and expectation. From Genesis to Revelation we see HOPE showing up and turning traumatic situations around for the glory of God.
    HOPE is a transporter. It transports you from death to life, from darkness to Light, from confusion to peace, from sadness to gladness, from sorrow to joy from sickness to wholeness. When you declare with your mouth "I have HOPE", everything in your life has to shift for better. Know it! Expect it! Receive it!

Romans 15:1 (NLT) I pray that God, the source of hope, will fill you completely with joy and peace because you trust in him. Then you will overflow with confident hope through the power of the Holy Spirit.

Day 2

HOPE'S Belief

A belief is faith, trust or confidence in someone or something. I have HOPE because my trust is in the Lord. Psalm 71; 5 (KJV) *"says For thou art my hope, O Lord God: thou art my trust from my youth."* God has proven himself to be trustworthy because he has always kept his word. His word is unshakable, unstoppable, unchangeable, and immutable. Today you can rest in the arms of a loving savior knowing that his words cannot and will not be altered.

I pray today that you have <u>confidence</u>. It is a reliable assurance that all things are working together for your good.

I pray today that you will have a <u>certainty</u> in your spirit. From this day on you will not allow doubt to take up residence in your life. What God has promised; he will make his word good.

I Pray today that your heart be guarded by the <u>conviction</u> HOPE brings. This conviction is rooted and grounded in the word of God and it cannot be undone.

I pray that God gives you <u>clarity</u> of thought, so that you can accurately declare the Word of Truth in every area of your life in Jesus name Amen.

Day 3

HOPE'S Expectation

The atmosphere of expectancy is the breeding ground of miracles. – Pastor Rod Parsley

My wife must be the Amazon queen. Every week we have packages being delivered. She loves Amazon because she has an Amazon Prime membership. Once you are amazon prime member, they will deliver your order within two days from your order date. If that package has not been left at the door. She will come in and grab the mailbox key because she knows the package is in the mailbox. She walks to the mailbox with expectancy in her heart and returns to the house with a package in her hand.

Some of you pray and ask God to do certain things but in your heart you don't expect it to manifest. Some of you believe that he will do it but you don't look for it to happen. HOPE says not only do I believe, but also I expect it to happen. You have to wait patiently with great expectation, knowing that what The Word of God has order for your life will be delivered. You have to rehearse the Word of God daily with anticipation knowing that it is on the way. The Bible declares in Psalm 62:5 (KJV) *My soul, wait thou only upon God; for my expectation is from him.*

Pray with me:
Father I thank you today because my day will be filled with expectation. I am eagerly expecting your promises to be made manifest in my life. I declare this shall be a day of miracles in Jesus name Amen.

Day 4

HOPE'S Focus

Romans 4:19-21(KJV)

19 *And being not weak in faith, he considered not his own body now dead, when he was about an hundred years old, neither yet the deadness of Sarah's womb:*
20 *He staggered not at the promise of God through unbelief; but was strong in faith, giving glory to God;*
21 *And being fully persuaded that, what he had promised, he was able also to perform.*

I love the story of Abraham and Sarah. Could you imagine being one hundred years old and waiting for a promise that was given so many years before that? Abraham had to come to this resolution. That he would keep his eyes on the promise and not allow anything to alter his focus.

The interesting fact is the scriptures said Abraham didn't even consider his age or the deadness of Sarah's womb. When you have locked onto HOPE's focus, you come to a new level of consciousness. The forces around you cannot shake this level of consciousness. The depth of Abraham's focus was to the point that he couldn't even doubt, criticize or negatively dispute what God had said. As a matter of fact he grew stronger in his faith. When you focus on the promise it will supply you with supernatural strength to give birth to what God has spoken.

Decree this with me:
I shall obtain every promise that God has spoken over My Life!
I am a winner!
I shall not doubt in My Heart!
I Believe and Expect every promise that is spoken over my life to Manifest Now In Jesus name Amen!

Day 5

HOPE'S Attitude

"Your attitude, not your aptitude, will determine your Altitude"- Zig Ziglar

Attitude is everything! Some of the greatest people to be around are people with a loving and contagious attitude. When you run into these types of people you always leave smiling and encouraged, with your head held high.

Attitude can be described, as a position or posture of the body appropriate to or expressive of an action or emotion. HOPE has an attitude that reeks of optimism. Optimism says I choose to believe that a good outcome will ultimately predominate in every situation. Optimism has a tendency to look favorably at every thing that is thrown its way.

Pessimism is the opposite of Optimism. Pessimism tends to expect the worst and maintains a negative disposition. Life is all about choices. You can choose to be pessimistic and expect the worst or you can choose to stand on the word of God and expect the best. Romans 12:2 (NLT) "Don't copy the behavior and customs of this world, but let God transform you into a new person by changing the way you think. Then you will learn to know God's will for you, which is good and pleasing and perfect." Your thoughts are a direct reflection of what you feed your mind. A constant diet and intake of the Word of God will keep you living with an attitude of HOPE. Recognize that a sovereign God lives on the inside of you and he will keep you from crippling pessimism.

Pray with me:
Jesus today I surrender my will, intellect, emotions to you. I thank you for you renewing my mind and giving me the power to Remain HOPEFUL no matter what I face with today in Jesus name I pray Amen.

Day 6

HOPE's Confidence

Numbers 23:19 (KJV) God is not a man, that he should lie; neither the son of man, that he should repent: hath he said, and shall he not do it? or hath he spoken, and shall he not make it good?

I will never forget I was 11 years old and I went to summer camp at Kids Across America in the Ozark Mountains. I had the time of my life that week. I made so many friends, and we played and worship and learned together. It was one the best experiences of my life. One day during our morning session we played a game called trust. Trust is where you climb up on this tree and you have to fall back and let your teammates catch you. Oh I knew I was going to be ok because Big D from Cincinnati was cool with everyone. But I was a little chunky and bigger than the rest of the guys. I climbed up and fell back and all of my teammates ran back and let me fall, leaving the camp counselors to run up and catch my head. I couldn't believe that teammates would let me fall.

Having confidence in the Word of God sometimes feels like your playing the game trust. You fall back trusting that God's word will not let you fall. Often times your emotions will run wild, causing you to think that things will never change. The bible declares in Jude 1:24 (KJV) *"Now unto him that is able to keep you from falling, and to present you faultless before the presence of his glory with exceeding joy. The Word of God will not let you Fall."*

HOPE's confidence is built upon the track record of the word of God. We have 66 books of the Bible that prove time after time that God will keep his word, and will not let his people fail. I know you have heard this. If he has done it before, he can and he will do it again. So go ahead and fall back and let his word catch you!

Declare with me: Today I have Godfidence!

Day 7

HOPE'S Confession

Hebrews 10:23(NASB) Let us hold fast the confession of our hope without wavering, for He who promised is faithful;

Your life is a divine reflection of the words you confess over yourself. The book of Proverbs tells us that life and death are in the power of the tongue. The hardest member of the body to tame is your tongue. What do you find yourself confessing over your life, ministry, work and family? Many times we pray one thing and then when we finish praying, we cancel out the things we prayed for by confessing the opposite of what we prayed. Every word that proceeds out of your mouth needs to reflect the HOPE you possess.

We are made in the image and likeness of God. The bible declares in Hebrews 11:3 (NKJV) *"By faith we understand that the worlds were framed by the word of God, so that the things which are seen were not made of things which are visible."* God framed the world we live in by his words. The word framed means to align or set in motion or make complete. The words that you confess frame your world, they align or set your days into motion. The same speaking creative power that's on the inside of God resides in you. Confess HOPE or the change you desire and watch it become your reality. I've come to declare to you today, that your life will rise to the level of your confession!

Pray with me:

Father I repent of every negative word or every word curse that I have spoken over my life. Today I ask you Father to change the way that I speak by renewing my mind with your Word. Father, ultimately let the words of my mouth and the meditations of my heart be acceptable in your sight in Jesus name amen.

Day 8

HOPE'S Scriptures

Romans 15:13 (KJV) Now the God of hope fill you with all joy and peace in believing, that ye may abound in hope, through the power of the Holy Ghost.

Romans 4:18 (KJV) Who against hope believed in hope, that he might become the father of many nations, according to that which was spoken, So shall thy seed be.

Romans 5:1-5 (KJV) Therefore being justified by faith, we have peace with God through our Lord Jesus Christ: **2** By whom also we have access by faith into this grace wherein we stand, and rejoice in hope of the glory of God. **3** And not only so, but we glory in tribulations also: knowing that tribulation worketh patience; **4** And patience, experience; and experience, hope: **5** And hope maketh not ashamed; because the love of God is shed abroad in our hearts by the Holy Ghost which is given unto us.

1 Peter 1:3 (KJV) Blessed be the God and Father of our Lord Jesus Christ, which according to his abundant mercy hath begotten us again unto a lively hope by the resurrection of Jesus Christ from the dead,

Philippians 1:20 (KJV) According to my earnest expectation and my hope, that in nothing I shall be ashamed, but that with all boldness, as always, so now also Christ shall be magnified in my body, whether it be by life, or by death.

Joshua 1:8-9 (KJV) **8** This book of the law shall not depart out of thy mouth; but thou shalt meditate therein day and night, that thou mayest observe to do according to all that is written therein: for then thou shalt make thy way prosperous, and then thou shalt have good success. **9** Have not I commanded thee? Be strong and of a good courage; be not afraid, neither be thou dismayed: for the Lord thy God is with thee whithersoever thou goest.

Psalm 62:5 (KJV) My soul, wait thou only upon God; for my expectation is from him. **3** John 1:2 (KJV) Beloved, I wish above all things that thou mayest prosper and be in health, even as thy soul prospereth.

Galatians 6:9 (KJV) And let us not be weary in well doing: for in due season we shall reap, if we faint not.

2 Corinthians 2:14 (New Life Version) We thank God for the power Christ has given us. He leads us and makes us win in everything. He speaks through us wherever we go. The Good News is like a sweet smell to those who hear it

Day 9

HOPE'S Cleansing

Hope is fragile and needs to be tended and renewed. - Patric Shad

There are times in life where you are drained and feel hopeless and need to be refreshed and renewed. Jewish people participate in a ritual of submersing themselves in a pool of "living waters" called the *"mikvah."* The word *mikvah* is defined as "a collection of living waters" or "HOPE." Some Jewish scholars define it as a pool of living HOPE. Jewish women would submerge themselves in the *Mikvah* to renew their reproductive rites. They would also use the *mikvah* as a place purification to wash off the old so they could embrace the new. Sometimes you need to allow HOPE to wash off the issues, pains and the debris from your past. Jewish scholars believe once you have immersed yourself with HOPE, you will have a renewed expectation and a fresh start. Ask the Holy Spirit to saturate you with fresh and give you a fresh start.

Lets pray this together:

Dear Jesus Wash me and restore the decayed areas of my life. Today I surrender to your will and I come into agreement with your plan for my life. Today is a day renewal and I'm walking into my fresh start in Jesus name amen.

Day 10

HOPE'S Anger

Ephesians 4:26 (NCV) When you are angry, do not sin, and be sure to stop being angry before the end of the day.

"Hope has two beautiful daughters; their names are Anger and Courage. Anger at the way things are, and Courage to see that they do not remain as they are." — *Augustine of Hippo*

Anger is a real emotion that some people try to skip over. Anger is a strong feeling of annoyance and displeasure for something or having a lack of tolerance. If we are honest with ourselves there are certain areas of our lives, businesses, ministries, families that have caused such anger to rise within us. IT'S REALLY OK! I choose to believe that when such feelings arise within you, that you do not have to settle or succumb to what's being presented to you.

So, lets be honest with ourselves and say "I'm angry at the way things are in my life!" Now the question is what are you going to do with that anger? What will be your response? Will you sit there and be an oasis of negativity and poison? Will you react violently and argumentatively and forcing people away from you? Or will you allow this pressure to become the energy that will produce positive changes in your life. Seize the moment and allow this anger to fuel your next steps towards greatness.

"May your choices reflect your hopes, not your fears." — *Nelson Mandela*

Dear Jesus I thank you today for the fruit of the spirit, which is *self-control,* is operating in my life. I have the discipline and strength to make the positive moves that will guide me closer to my destiny. I love you Lord so much that I will not allow my anger to break your heart. Let all my actions be pleasing in your sight in Jesus name I pray amen.

Day 11

HOPE'S Courage

"Hope has two beautiful daughters; their names are Anger and Courage. Anger at the way things are, and Courage to see that they do not remain as they are." — Augustine of Hippo

Joshua 1:9 (NLT) This is my command—be strong and courageous! Do not be afraid or discouraged. For the Lord your God is with you wherever you go.

Anger is the fuel to provoke to change. But Courage is the driving force that enables a person to see that those changes become a reality. The definition of courage is the quality of mind that enables a person to face difficulty.

I love Joshua Chapter 1 because there you see God commissioning Joshua to go over the Jordan and to take the people to the promise land. One of the biggest enemies of progression is fear. Fear is a debilitating emotion that keeps people in bondage to their current dilemma. Once you recognize that you are battling fear, you have to release the power of the Holy Spirit to give you the Courage to see that you do not remain in your current place. Remember fear is a feeling but it's not your destiny.

For the next season of your life don not allow fear and discouragement to imprison you. You have to remind yourself daily you have the Courage, strength, power and victorious mindset to come out of every dilemma and to accomplish every goal.

Declare this over yourself:
Ephesians 3:20 (KJV) Now unto him that is able to do exceeding abundantly above all that we ask or think, according to the power that worketh in us.

" I HAVE THE POWER!"

Day 12

HOPE'S Joy

Nehemiah 8:10 (NLT) And Nehemiah[a] continued, "Go and celebrate with a feast of rich foods and sweet drinks, and share gifts of food with people who have nothing prepared. This is a sacred day before our Lord. Don't be dejected and sad, for the joy of the Lord is your strength!"

I've often heard happiness is caused by happenings. A lot of times you've search for sources of inspiration or happiness in the wrong areas. Your only source of True Joy comes from God. When HOPE permeates your being it releases new levels of Joy. This Joy gives you an ability to cheer up and be glad no matter what's taking place in your life. The reason you are able to be glad is, because you know change is on the way. Expectation releases joy that cause an overwhelming sense of gratitude.

The Bible declares his strength is made perfect in my weakness. This means the Joy of The Lord will carry you to an expected destination.

Declare this scripture over yourself:

Habakkuk 3:18 (NLT)

Yet I will rejoice in the Lord! I will be joyful in the God of my salvation!

Day 13

HOPE'S Peace

Peace is not an emotion, but it is a place you choose to live. – Pastor Pat Schatzline

That is a powerful quote. The first time I heard my mentor Pastor Pat say peace is a place I live, I said to myself, I'm changing my address. Pastor Pat says, *"Each day I draw a circle around myself and declare in this space peace reigns."* So many times we allow our emotions to dictate and control our state of mind. But you have to learn to silence your emotions and declare that God is in control. You have to declare the word of God in Jeremiah 29:11 (KJV) **"For I know the thoughts that I think toward you, saith the Lord, thoughts of peace, and not of evil, to give you an expected end."** Today is the day that you declare that it is well with your soul. You have to rest knowing that God has already worked everything out for your good. Change your living situation and move into a place called **PEACE**.

Recite This:

I'm somewhere in my future and it looks much better than it looks right now. – Pastor Brenda Ray

Day 14

HOPE'S Perspective

To imagine things other than they are is the essence of HOPE. It is also the stuff of revolution. – Leonard Sweet

I know you have heard this saying countless of times, "Everything begins in the mind." Perspective is the mental capacity or the mental outlook on something. The change that you are HOPEING for has to become a reality in your mind first. Your mind is the birthing room to your future and destiny. I never forget when my son Kaleb was being born. My wife told me, "Mr. McKinney I will not allow everyone including family and friends into the birthing room." You have to protect your mind and keep it sterilized like a birthing room.

Getting to a better place in life is like riding in a car to particular destination. You can choose to view life through the windshield of fresh and new possibilities. Or you can choose to stare at the rear view mirror of defeat. I recall Bishop Harold Calvin Ray use to tell us weekly, *"Destiny is not a matter of chance but a matter or Choice."* Allow your mind to give birth to New and wonderful possibilities.

"You cannot swim for new horizons until you have courage to lose sight of the shore."
— *William Faulkner*

Pray with me:

Dear Jesus Transform every area of my life by renewing my mind. Today my thoughts will give birth to the seeds of the word of God. Lord protect my mind from every evil and deadly thought. Today I embrace the dawning of a new beginning in Jesus name amen.

Day 15
HOPE Dealers

Plant seeds of happiness, hope, success, and love; it will all come back to you in abundance. This is the law of nature." — *Steve Maraboli*

Romans 15:13 (NLT) I pray that God, the source of hope, will fill you completely with joy and peace because you trust in him. Then you will overflow with confident hope through the power of the Holy Spirit.

I'll never forget I was 13 years old and I was pumping gas for my grandmother. This particular gas pump didn't have the cut-off mechanism to keep the gasoline from overflowing. So I just let the gas flow and then I turned around and gasoline was flowing everywhere. I looked down and I was standing in a puddle of gas. As HOPE dealers everywhere we go we should overflow with HOPE. We are responsible for leaving people inspired with HOPE. The Holy Spirit does not fill you up to overflow on yourself. The purpose of the overflow is for you to share HOPE with a hopeless generation. My prayer for you is that God will make you magnetic and that people will be drawn to you, to receive HOPE. When you lay down at night you should ask yourself a question. Lord did I make an impact today and leave people HOPEFUL?

Pray this Prayer:
Jesus today as I go out let me come into contact with people that are broken, crushed, sick and feeling hopeless. Lord fill me up with HOPE so I can share HOPE with them. Help me to awaken the HOPE you have placed within them. Amen.

Day 16

HOPE'S Foundation

Colossians 1:27 (KJV) To whom God would make known what is the riches of the glory of this mystery among the Gentiles; which is Christ in you, the hope of glory:

Christ Jesus came to the earth to be HOPE for the world. He conquered death, hell and the grave. Jesus of Nazareth is the Unstoppable King of kings and Lord of lords. When you received Christ Jesus into your life, you plugged into an unlimited power supply that never fails. From the decree of Herod to kill all of the children under two years old, to enduring the most brutal crucifixion known to all mankind. None of these things could stop him.

He came to be our HOPE that could not be stopped. I love the scripture in Acts 17:28(KJV) *"For in him we live, and move, and have our being; as certain also of your own poets have said, For we are also his offspring."* Because you're in Christ and Christ is you, you have abounding HOPE. What is Apostle Paul saying in Colossians 1:27? The word Christ signifies he is the anointed one or empowered one. The Anointed one that lives in you is the foundation of your HOPE. You are not unstoppable in your own strength. But your life is a testimony of the unstoppable power of God.

Jesus you are amazing and I thank you for making me victorious like you. Thank you Lord that you have equipped me with the power to be unstoppable. Today I rejoice because HOPE is alive and well in me right now in the name of Jesus amen.

Day 17

Unstoppable HOPE

"Hope, it is the only thing stronger than fear. A little hope is effective, a lot of hope is dangerous." — *Suzanne Collins*

2 Corinthians 2:14 (KJV) Now thanks be unto God, which always causeth us to triumph in Christ, and maketh manifest the savour of his knowledge by us in every place.

I want you to understand one thing. Because HOPE is alive in you, you cannot be defeated. Sickness, poverty, stress and sorrow cannot hold you captive when HOPE is on the inside of you. The HOPE that resides in you is dangerous. That's why the devil attempts to steal, kill and destroy you but he can't. The Bible declares in 1 John 4:4 (King James Version) "Ye are of God, little children, and have overcome them: because greater is he that is in you, than he that is in the world."

HOPE makes you become more than a conqueror. HOPE supernaturally infuses you with the strength to soar with the eagles and run with the horses. HOPE enables you with the power to triumph over anything that comes your way. God created you to win and overcome in life. HOPE is unbeatable, unshakable, and most of all it is Unstoppable!!

Father I thank you for making me a winner. Today I declare everything that has been sent to stop me is bound in operable in Jesus name! I walk in the authority of Christ Jesus and every area of my life is winning in Jesus name amen.

Day 18

Declarations of HOPE

I am Fearfully and Wonderfully made in the image of God.

I am created anew in Christ Jesus.

I am God's Masterpiece.

I am an Ambassador of the Kingdom of God.

My past is behind me and I am pressing on to fulfill my purpose.

I am empowered by the Holy Spirit.

I am protected from hurt and harm.

I am covered in the blood of Jesus.

I am created to win and excel in life.

I am a Kingdom Agent spreading HOPE everywhere that I go.

I am a Hilarious giver.

I am Free from Defeat and negativity.

I am off limits from every demonic attack that is formed against me.

I am chosen by the Grace of God.

I am healed and free from all sickness and disease.

I am equipped to accomplish every goal.

I posses everything I need to be successful.

I am a conduit of the Joy of the Lord.

I am free from every generational curse.

I am blessed to bless others.

I have a victorious mentality.

I am blessed to produce cutting-edge concepts and ideas.

I possess the spirit of excellence.

I walk in forgiveness.

I am free from the curse of lack and poverty.

I am favored by God.

I am healthy emotionally, physically and spiritually.

I am Unstoppable!

www.ingramcontent.com/pod-product-compliance
Lightning Source LLC
LaVergne TN
LVHW050046090426
835510LV00043B/3329